On Saturday April 15th 1989 a fatal crush occurred on the terraces of the Hillsborough football stadium in Sheffield. It was, and remains to this day, the worst tragedy in British sporting history, as 96 people died and hundreds more were injured.

The Disaster became known simply as **'Hillsborough'.**

What follows is a reconstruction of the key events that led to, and caused, the Disaster. The history of official investigations, as well as the legal pursuit by victims' families, is also detailed.

The information and findings that emerged from those events are concisely reported herein.

These are, then, the important facts from before, during and after the Disaster.

GW00501480

Foreword

When disasters happen, the sheer scale, confusion and trauma of the 'moment' overwhelm all involved: the dying, the injured, the survivors, the witnesses and the authorities. No-one should be content with pointing the finger of blame at those who make errors of judgement in the heat of the moment.

Yet, when institutional complacency and gross negligence by those in positions of power contribute to the circumstances of disaster, from the failure to respond effectively to the emergency, and the treatment of the bereaved and survivors, and to deceitful allegations that attempt to shift responsibility onto the victims and their families, we are dealing with an entirely different issue. When the processes of investigation and inquiry not only fail to deliver even the basic elements of natural justice but also collude to mask the truth and deny culpability, we have to question their role within a society that prides itself on its democratic principles and its rule of law.

The deaths of 96 men, women and children at Hillsborough, the hundreds of those injured and the thousands traumatised, are the tip of an iceberg of grief and suffering among friends and families. Each year at Anfield on 15th April, thousands stand together on the Kop to share in a collective tribute to those who set out on a beautiful spring day to watch a football match, never to return.

The Disaster unfolded in front of television cameras, was recorded on CCTV, and happened in the presence of hundreds of journalists; yet soon after, the myths of Hillsborough consolidated around blaming the fans for forcing entry, being drunk and violent and, to paraphrase Brian Clough, killing their own people. Emanating from a lie told by the South Yorkshire Police Match Commander, while fans were being pulled from the terraces, the lens of hooliganism has continued to dominate commentaries on Hillsborough 20 years on. With the media so heavily represented how has this myth been sustained?

"Hillsborough: Context and Consequences" sets about answering that question, and many others. It provides an informed, well-constructed and accessible account of the background to the Disaster, what happened in the build-up and the emergency responses. It covers the aftermath and the failures of the lengthy legal processes in establishing responsibility. It lends emphasis to the Home Office inquiry that identified overcrowding as the main cause and police mismanagement of the crowd as the main reason. What follows is an overview of the key issues, easily read, yet fully referenced. It is an invaluable, educative resource for those seeking a clear understanding of the injustices of Hillsborough.

Regrettably, it is necessary to do this because the myths of Hillsborough live on, leaving the bereaved and survivors still, after 20 years, defending their reputations and those of their loved ones. In itself, this serves as a reminder that injustice was the tragedy that arose out of the Hillsborough Disaster. It is an indictment of the 'justice system' that after two decades no-one has been held responsible institutionally or individually for the disaster or the cover-up that followed. There has been no acknowledgement of responsibility and no apology. What follows contributes significantly to putting the record straight.

Phil Scraton
Professor of Criminology
Institute of Criminology and Criminal Justice
School of Law
Queens University
Belfast
February 2009

Acknowledgements

The production of this document would not have been possible without the invaluable assistance, inspiration and input of many individuals.

Just like the 96, none of them will be forgotten.

Our respective better halves, often neglected during writing but nonetheless always worthy muses:
Liam O'Mahony
Joanne Sharman

Feedback & assistance:
Sheila Coleman
Sarah Deane
Phil Hammond
Michael Hines
Amanda Jacks
Damian Kavanagh
Bob McCluskey
Phil Scraton
Dave Smith
Wendy White
Anne Williams

We thank the staff at "Red And White Kop" for all their assistance in taking the project forward from an initial internet forum post to what it is today. For much assistance with design, layout and formatting, we especially thank the following:
Alan Farlie
Mike Turner

We also thank all the staff at LiverpoolFC.tv for their work in assisting us to promote the project and for all their help in contacting various journalists and other media sources. Here we especially thank the following:
Matt Owen
Matt Walker

Finally we owe a huge debt of gratitude to all the individuals and companies for their contributions that allowed this work to be published, especially Mark at CDP Print Management for organising the subsidy.

Further information and discussion can be found on the following links:

www.hfdinfo.com
www.facebook.com/group.php?gid=12210106214

If you wish, you can contact us through the main website's email address with any queries:

feedback@hfdinfo.com

First published by Em-Project Limited in partnership with 'hfdinfo', in Great Britain 2009.
©2009 the authors.

Printed by CDP Print Management.

Designed by Em-Project Limited.

A catalogue record for this book is available from the British Library ISBN 978-0-9562275-0-8

Grounds For Concern

The Hillsborough Disaster of 1989 was by no means the first time football supporters had encountered problems at this specific ground. The turnstiles frequently could not cope with the number of people awaiting admittance and, inside the ground, there were recurrent incidents of crushing at the Leppings Lane End.

The first recorded incident took place in 1981 during the Football Association (FA) Cup semi-final fixture between Wolverhampton Wanderers Football Club (Wolves) and Tottenham Hotspur Football Club (Spurs). In spite of having a larger average following, Spurs' supporters were given fewer tickets than Wolves' and were also allocated the 10,100 capacity Leppings Lane End.

Within minutes of the game starting a crush developed in the stand and 38 Spurs supporters were injured. On this occasion the police allowed the affected supporters access to the pitch.

Following this incident the FA opted to select other venues to host FA Cup semi-finals for the next six years. Stadium owners, Sheffield Wednesday Football Club (SWFC), were prompted to make significant changes to the Leppings Lane End. South Yorkshire Police (SYP) suggested a reduction in overall capacity[1] and the division of terraces into sections. The idea was that the capacity could be distributed equally and evenly across the terrace. Lateral fences were erected on the terrace to create five penned areas.

Despite these changes, there was no reassessment of Leppings Lane's capacity. The individual pen capacities were carved from the 10,100 figure. There was neither any system to count the number of fans entering each pen nor any system to warn when a pen had reached its capacity. New ideas were drafted to resolve these issues but never implemented. With no count system, SWFC was in breach of its safety certificate at every single match.[2]

It was not until 1987, that problems resurfaced, when the FA reselected Hillsborough to host the FA Cup semi-final. *"There was evidence that the central pens were uncomfortably overcrowded on that occasion and again at the 1988 Cup semi-final."*[3]

Prior to both the '88 and '89 games, Liverpool Football Club (LFC) challenged the decision to allocate the smaller terrace section to their supporters, while the enormous 'Kop' stand went to Nottingham Forest Football Club (NFFC).

---

1   The Interim Taylor Report, paragraph 124.
2   David Conn, "The Beautiful Game: Searching the Soul of Football", page 94.
3   The Interim Taylor Report, paragraph 181.

The first objection in 1988 was due to the size of the allocation. The second objection in 1989 was due to the complaints that LFC received from its supporters, who had experienced crushing in 1988.

Despite the grounds for concern, Hillsborough was once again selected to host the 1989 FA Cup semi-final match between LFC and NFFC.

The Liverpool End
SYP advised the FA regarding which end of the ground should be given to which set of supporters, as they had done in 1987 and 1988.

For so-called *"safety reasons"*[4] SYP repeated in 1989 the ticket and turnstile allocations of the '88 semi-final, with LFC being allocated the north and west stands, NFFC the south and east stands.

Just as in the previous year, LFC supporters were once again given fewer tickets than their opponents. Their allocation was 24,000 tickets whereas NFFC's was 29,000 tickets.

LFC's supporters were able to access the stadium through just 23 turnstiles, whereas NFFC supporters had access through 60 turnstiles.

Turnstile Admission
The 60 turnstiles allocated to NFFC ran the full length of two sides of the ground, whereas LFC's turnstiles were all situated at one corner end.

The pressure therefore to admit the given number of LFC supporters was greater at these turnstiles. *"In 1986, a police memorandum written to senior officers warned that the Leppings Lane turnstiles don't provide anything like the access required."*[5] That observation went unheeded and admission to the ground once again proved difficult for supporters.

Although the Leppings Lane End turnstiles were labelled alphabetically, they did not run in that order, making it hard to follow the directions on the tickets. In addition, there were insufficient numbers of police officers at hand to direct supporters or organise queues.

Admission rates proceeded to fall while congestion outside the turnstiles developed and grew as more fans arrived.

4   Brian Reade, "Living With The Same Bird For 43 Years", page 172.
5   Phil Scraton, "Hillsborough: The Truth", page 46.

Finding Their Own Level

Supporters who had passed through the turnstiles were left to find their own way to the terraces.

The option of filling the five pens successively had been rejected by senior officers. Earlier in the day, Superintendent Bernard Murray told Chief Inspector Creaser that supporters should be left to *"find their own level"*.[6]

With no direction, supporters found that the *"obvious"*[7] route to the terrace was via a tunnel. Above the tunnel entrance was the word 'standing'. Most standing supporters presumed this was the only route to the terrace. Many were unaware that there were two other points of access.

There were *"no conspicuous signs"*[7] to invite supporters to take the alternative routes. Supporters were *"drawn to the tunnel"*,[7] which led to only two of the five available pens – the central pens.

The Central Pens

The official combined capacity figure for the central pens was 2,200.[8] Later the Health & Safety Executive (HSE) found that figure was too high.

The combined capacity figure should have been reduced to 1,600, as the crush barriers installed did not conform to paragraph 142 in 'The Guide to Safety at Sport 1986.'

Even Distribution Of Supporters

SYP *"hoped"*[9] that even distribution would be achieved, instead of taking action to guarantee it. They reasoned that, by leaving all pens open, the supporters would eventually level themselves out.

Chief Superintendent David Duckenfield, the officer in overall charge that day, assumed any supporters finding the central pens too crowded would be able *"to turn around and walk out"*.[10] In theory, those fans would then fill up the emptier pens and distribution would be achieved.

There was, however, only one way for fans to exit the central pens and that was to go back through, against the flow of incoming supporters, the same access tunnel which was 40ft in length, dark and had a slope steeper than the 'Green Guide' stipulated.

---

6   The Interim Taylor Report, paragraph 58.
7   The Interim Taylor Report, paragraph 44.
8   The Interim Taylor Report, paragraph 126.
9   The Interim Taylor Report, paragraph 171.
10   Phil Scraton, "Hillsborough: The Truth", page 63.

The option to leave was made more difficult when a police tannoy announcement requested that supporters in the central pens should move forward so as to make room for others. By 2:30pm the option was completely gone, as many supporters within the pens and in the tunnel itself had lost voluntary control of their direction.

At this point, Duckenfield noted that the central pens were *"getting on for being quite full"*.[11] Still, no order was given to direct supporters to the emptier pens. At the subsequent public inquiry, the SYP argued that, although it was common practice to monitor and close access to pens at league matches, at FA Cup semi-finals the pens were left open.[12]

That argument can be rejected easily due to the fact SYP monitored, closed access to, and *"successfully"*[13] distributed supporters across the terraces at the '88 semi-final. Mr Lock, SWFC's Security Officer and a former policeman, said, *"It would have been quite easy to close the centre pens to ensure people were moved to the side pens."*

Duckenfield admitted that following this procedure was something that *"didn't cross his mind."*[14] He had only been appointed 21 days before the match, had no recent experience in policing such a high profile match and the procedure had not featured in the previous year's planning.

As a result, numbers in the central pens continued to swell, whilst the wing pens remained relatively empty. BBC match commentator, John Motson, noticed the disparity in the pens and made reference to the lack of fans in the wing areas. Unbeknown to him, there were a substantial number of fans still outside, awaiting admittance.

"Open The Gate!"
Outside the turnstiles, the congestion had grown so severe that there was a perceived risk to life. In 1987, when congestion arose at the same turnstiles due to supporters arriving late, SYP decided to delay kick-off.

Duckenfield, however, decided against this course of action even though it was requested by PC Buxton, who believed a delayed kick-off would immediately reduce the pressure.[15] At 2:47pm a request was made to open an exit gate. Five minutes later, Duckenfield agreed to open the gate.

11   Phil Scraton, "Hillsborough: The Truth", page 62.
12   The Interim Taylor Report, paragraph 171.
13   The Interim Taylor Report, paragraph 270.
14   The Interim Taylor Report, paragraph 229.
15   The Interim Taylor Report, paragraphs 62, 65 & 226.

SYP later argued that although they had five minutes to sort how the influx of fans would be absorbed, they did not do so because they could not have foreseen the outcome.[16]

Several witnesses refute this and testified that warnings were given to officers wanting to open the gates. One officer was reportedly told by a steward, *"No way! There'll be a crush in there!"*

Turnstile attendant, Colin Milton, said the officer ignored the steward's warning.[17] Another SWFC steward, Jack Stone, who had been asked four times for the keys to open Exit Gate A, but refused each time, said in his own statement, *"I knew all hell would be let loose if the gates were opened."*[18]

Gate C was opened and, for five minutes, there was an influx of 2,000 supporters into the stadium. Undoubtedly opening the gate relieved the pressure outside but, with no directive to do otherwise, the majority of supporters headed for the tunnel leading to the central pens.

Lord Justice Taylor said the decision to open the gate, with no attempt to steer fans to the emptier wing pens, was *"a blunder of the first magnitude."*[19]

The Notion Of Inrushing Supporters
It is a commonly-held belief that the thousands of Liverpool supporters who entered via Gate C then rushed into the back of the already-overfull central pens, with the effect that those supporters at the front were crushed to death (the BBC's Politics Show on 2/12/07 contains the latest example of this supposition. The BBC has since had to apologise for this, as there was never any evidence to support the view expressed).

CCTV evidence clearly showed supporters entering via Gate C walking across the concourse and into the tunnel. Taylor revealed that, of those who died near the front of the pens, *"at least 16 and probably 21"*[20] came through Gate C after it had been opened at 2:52pm.

It was estimated that, with the addition of supporters from Gate C, there were more than 3,000 fans in the central pens, almost double the official capacity.

16   The Interim Taylor Report, paragraph 229.
17   Martin Sharpe, The Sun, April 17th 1989, page 9.
18   Peter Davenport/David Sapstead in The Times newspaper. We have not been able to confirm the date, as our
        original url is now a dead link, although we are certain the quotation is correct.
19   The Interim Taylor Report, paragraph 231.
20   The Interim Taylor Report, paragraph 108.

The Crush
The lateral fences prevented supporters from escaping to the spacious wing pens, whilst the fences at the front prevented any escape to the pitch. The influx of supporters from the tunnel prevented a retreat backwards.

With nowhere to go, the pressure built up slowly and increased with each passing minute. Survivor Eddie Spearitt described the crush as being *"like a vice, getting tighter and tighter."*[21]

The intensity of the crush was most severe towards the front of the pens, where the great majority of victims received their fatal injuries, but there *"were a few fatalities further back."*[22]

As a result of the crush, 730 supporters were injured; 96 fatally.[23]

The Emergency Response
The emergency response began only when Liverpool supporters spilled on to the pitch and the match was brought to an abrupt end at 3:06pm.

The Liverpool Supporters' Reaction
LFC supporters were first to react to the unfolding Disaster. In the upper tier of the West Stand, supporters reached down and pulled fellow supporters out of the Leppings Lane End pens.

Supporters also tried to administer first aid and used advertising boards as make-shift stretchers to ferry away the injured. Taylor described the efforts of these supporters as *"magnificent."*[24]

Police In The Control Room
In the Control Room, police had access to five CCTV screens, all receiving live images from the cameras situated around the ground. All cameras had zoom capability and were fully functioning on the day of the Disaster.

Officers could view the area ahead of the turnstiles, the concourse inside the ground, individual pens and the people inside them. Additionally, the Control Room was perfectly situated to allow officers to view the Leppings Lane End with the naked eye.[25]

21   Brian Reade, "Living With The Same Bird For 43 Years", page 174.
       "The Lost Afternoon", The Guardian April 11th 1999
       Full account of Eddie Spearritt's experience can be found in P. Scraton's "Hillsborough: The Truth."
22   The Interim Taylor Report, paragraphs 108 & 111.
23   The Interim Taylor Report, paragraph 121.
24   The Interim Taylor Report, paragraph 125.
25   The Interim Taylor Report, paragraph 170 / The Stuart-Smith Scrutiny Report, chapter 2, paragraph 42.

Furthermore, radio contact with officers around the ground was possible and indeed radio transmissions of distress and possible injuries were heard by SYP Headquarters, who then phoned the Control Room at 2:59pm to ask if any ambulances were needed.

The Control Room responded that there were *"no reports of injuries",* but to stand by.[26] Control Room officers said afterwards that they believed a pitch invasion was occurring at first and that was why they requested operational support (a call for more police officers) and they also called for dog handlers.

At the inquiry, Taylor concluded that *"Duckenfield's capacity to take decisions and give orders seemed to collapse."*[27] Several vital minutes were wasted because Duckenfield *"froze".*[28]

It was not until 3:29pm that the emergency services were properly alerted to the Disaster. That was when the Major Disaster Vehicle (the only vehicle equipped to deal with large-scale incidents) was called for.

Pitch-Side Police Reaction

Five officers were stationed on the track in front of the Leppings Lane terraces. Their written instructions made no reference to the detection of overcrowding,[29] but their instructions did specify that supporters in need of medical attention should be allowed access to the pitch.

The sheer weight of people in the pens led to exit gates in the perimeter fence springing open. Officers prevented injured supporters from leaving the pens, contrary to their own instructions and to advice from Lord Justice Popplewell that *"in the event of an emergency, fans must be granted access to the pitch."*[30]

Pitch-side officers did, however, try to alert the ground's Control Room to the situation. With no response forthcoming, they eventually took the decision to open the gates and then tried to administer first aid. This was just one example of some officers acting on their own initiative.

Other junior officers ran round to the tunnel to try to relieve the pressure from that end.

---

26   The Interim Taylor Report, paragraphs 106.
27   The Interim Taylor Report, paragraph 282.
28   The Interim Taylor Report, paragraph 284.
29   The Interim Taylor Report, paragraph 245.
30   Lord Justice Popplewell, Committee of Inquiry into Crowd Safety & Control at Sports Grounds, Interim Report, Home Office cmnd 9585, paragraph 215.

Ground Commander, Superintendent Roger Greenwood, also acted without instruction when he ran on to the pitch to tell the match referee, Ray Lewis, to stop the game. Lewis immediately halted the game at 3:06pm and called the players off.

The stopping of the match, and the subsequent clearing of the playing surface, was crucial to allowing emergency services to come to the aid of the supporters. It also enabled other supporters to extricate the injured, dying and dead from the pens.

The Medical Response
Doctors at the ground also came on to the pitch of their own accord to assist the injured. They were joined by the 30 St John's Ambulance officers who were stationed around the ground.

They attempted to revive people through the perimeter fence and on the pitch. At 3:13pm, a St John's ambulance came on to the pitch and stationed itself by pens 3 & 4.

There was just one single South Yorkshire Metropolitan Ambulance Service (SYMAS) vehicle outside the ground, on stand-by.[31] It was not until 3:07pm that more ambulances were requested.

At 3:13pm a fleet of 42 ambulances started to arrive. However, they were prevented from entering the ground because SYP were still reporting *"crowd trouble"*.[32] When permission was finally granted, some twenty minutes later, the ambulances then had difficulty accessing the pitch due to the positioning of advertising boards and other changes made to the ground.[32]

Fire engines, carrying hydraulic cutting gear and resuscitation equipment, also had difficulty accessing the stadium. The fire-fighters were forced to carry their equipment into the ground. By the time they and the Major Disaster Vehicle arrived at 3:40pm, most supporters had left the pens.[33]

A number of emergency service officers at the ground, as well as various off-duty doctors and medics, heavily criticised the lack of organisation as well as poor communication and co-ordination of ensuring that adequate aid reached the injured and dying.

---

31   The Interim Taylor Report, paragraphs 105.
32   The Interim Taylor Report, paragraph 302.
33   The Interim Taylor Report, paragraph 101-104.

The Immediate Aftermath

In the end, only 14 of the 96 victims made it to a hospital; the rest were ferried to a nearby gymnasium, where they were laid out on the floor. At 3:45pm a doctor treating people on the pitch was asked to examine those in the gym and certify deaths. As the deaths were counted, erroneous reports began to circulate that supporters were responsible for the Disaster.

The Media View

The reporters at the ground knew there were *"simply too many fans at one end of the ground"*[34] but why this happened was an unanswered question. Shortly after the St John's ambulance arrived on the pitch, the press were given a possible explanation.

Graham Mackrell, SWFC's Secretary and Safety Officer, told media sources that a gate had been forced open and supporters had rushed in.

The press then interviewed the FA's Chief Executive, Graham Kelly, about this allegation, and the possibility of *"unauthorised entries"*[35] to the stadium was added to the emerging story.

By 4:00pm the reported cause of the Disaster was as follows: *"At ten to three there was a surge of fans at the Leppings Lane End of the ground. The surge composed of about 500 Liverpool fans and the police say that a gate was forced and that led to a crush in the terracing area."*[36]

This media explanation for the Disaster was relayed to millions, effectively forming the public perception and was based on what Lord Justice Stuart-Smith, in his later report, called *"a disgraceful lie."*[37]

Policing Opinion

Both Kelly and Mackrell had gone to the Police Control Room for information shortly after 3:15pm. There they were both *"misinformed and misled"*[38] by Duckenfield that a gate had been forced when in fact Duckenfield had ordered the gate to be opened. Taylor knew this meeting *"set off"*[39] the false reports that followed.

---

34   BBC Radio Two, 15/04/89.
35   Steve Lohr, New York Times, 16/04/89.
36   http://www.contrast.org/hillsborough/history/media.shtm
37   The Stuart-Smith Scrutiny Report, chapter 4, paragraph 100.
38   Phil Scraton, "Hillsborough: The Truth", page 66.
39   The Interim Taylor Report, paragraph 283.

However, even before this meeting, allegations that fans had caused the Disaster were being circulated from the Control Room. During a request for fence cutters, logged at 3:13pm, supporters were accused of breaking down a gate. The police version of events was only disproved when footage emerged from BBC cameras recording the scenes outside the turnstiles.

Even with this revelation, the police maintained supporter responsibility and accused supporters of deliberately creating the crisis at the turnstiles which forced officers to open the gate. Just like before, information that supporters were late, ticketless, drunk and unruly was passed to key spokespersons who then volunteered their opinion on the causes of the Disaster to the media.

"Late"
Chief Constable Peter Wright stated in a press conference later that evening; *"3,000 fans turned up in a ten minute period before kick-off."*[40]

Graham Mackrell also inferred on 'Match of the Day' that LFC supporters had arrived late.[41] The information on the tickets however, issued under Mackrell's supervision, requested fans to arrive 15 minutes prior to kick-off.[42]

SWFC's own admission count showed that 4,593 of the 10,100 supporters in Leppings Lane had entered the ground by 2:30pm.[43]

Taylor said that at 2:30pm, *"more than 5,000 fans were still awaiting admittance."*[44] He also concluded that the small area ahead of the turnstiles, of which there was an insufficient number, caused the congestion and therefore dismissed any conspiracy theory linked to a large number of late-arriving supporters.[45]

The HSE findings were key to Taylor's assessment. They concluded that the Leppings Lane turnstiles were likely to cause delays and crowd congestion.[46] They also estimated that there needed to be a continuous stream of admissions, at a rate of 700 per turnstile per hour, from 1:00pm onwards to have any chance of admitting 10,100 before kick-off.[47]

40 & 41   http://uk.youtube.com/watch?v=uaA1XHcDt7U
42 & 44   The Interim Taylor Report, paragraph 192.
43   http://www.hse.gov.uk/foi/releases/hillsborough/me8934.pdf
45   The Interim Taylor Report, paragraph 208.
46   Health & Safety Executive Report, paragraph 6.3.
47   Health & Safety Executive Report, paragraph 9.4.

Effectively 5,000 supporters needed to have entered the ground by 2:00pm to have any chance of admitting the remaining 5,000 before kick-off. Taylor surmised that *"both the police and the club should have realised that the Leppings Lane turnstiles and the waiting area outside would be under strain to admit all the Liverpool supporters in time."*[48]

"Ticketless"
Police Federation Officer Paul Middup, when interviewed by ITV, stated that *"500 plus"* were without tickets and were *"hell bent"* on getting in.[49]

Yet officers at the turnstiles denied there were a large number of ticketless supporters.[50] SWFC's own admission count system showed the terrace did not exceed its 10,100 capacity. The HSE also conclusively proved there was no substance to Middup's allegations.

As part of their analysis, the HSE counted the number of LFC supporters entering the ground, including those through the turnstiles, through Gate C and even those who climbed over the turnstiles. They gave three admission figures based on their analysis.

Their first figure was 9,267, their 'best estimate' was 9,734, and their third figure was a 'maximum estimate' of 10,124. The HSE report stated it was unlikely that the terrace exceeded 10,124 and that total admissions were approximately equal to the designated capacity of 10,100 people.[51]

Taylor surmised there was no substance to the allegation that ticketless fans caused the Disaster.[52]

"Drunk"
The day after the Disaster, Prime Minister Margaret Thatcher, her Press Secretary Bernard Ingham and Home Secretary Douglas Hurd were shown around the stadium by police officials.

Ingham told the press, *"I know what I learned on the spot: there would have been no Hillsborough if a mob, clearly tanked up, had not tried to force their way in."*[53]

---

48   The Interim Taylor Report, paragraph 190.
49   ITN News at 10, 18/04/89.
50   The Interim Taylor Report, paragraph 200.
51   Health & Safety Executive Report, paragraphs 5.8, 6.2, 8.1, The Interim Taylor Report, paragraphs 200-203.
52   The Interim Taylor Report, paragraph 208.
53   Phil Scraton, "Death On The Terraces", page 184.

Officers sought to find evidence to support this theory by collecting information on the amount of alcohol purchased from pubs and off-licences in the area before kick-off. Police had already interviewed bereaved families, immediately after they had identified their loved ones' bodies, to ascertain how much alcohol each of the deceased had drunk before the game.

The allegation of drunken fans also seemed to influence the Sheffield Coroner, who inexplicably decided to take blood alcohol levels from every victim, including a ten-year-old boy.[54]

Taylor considered the allegation but found drunkenness was not a contributing factor. Taylor said, *"The great majority were not drunk or even the worse for drink"*,[55] adding, *"Some officers, seeking to rationalise their loss of control, overestimated the drunkenness in the crowd."*[56]

"Aggressive"
The impression of aggressive behaviour had already been given visual credence: a line of police officers formed on the halfway line whilst the Disaster unfolded, as if to segregate LFC supporters from NFFC supporters. As LFC supporters spilled on to the pitch, *"John Motson recognised and made mention, well before the match was stopped, that the trouble seemed to be overcrowding and not misbehaviour."*[57] Yet the allegation persisted, grew and dominated press reports in the days following the Disaster.

Then, on April 19th 1989, The Sun newspaper published its now-infamous story entitled 'The Truth', with three sub-headlines which claimed: *"some fans picked pockets of victims"*, *"some fans urinated on the brave cops"* and *"some fans beat up PC giving the kiss of life."*

The story accompanying those headlines claimed *"drunken Liverpool fans viciously attacked rescue workers as they tried to revive victims"* and *"police officers, firemen and ambulance crew were punched, kicked and urinated upon."*

The story itself was based on comments made by Irvine Patnick, the MP for Sheffield Hallam, and an unnamed police officer.[58]

---

54   Phil Scraton, "Hillsborough: The Truth", page 88.
55 & 56 The Interim Taylor Report, paragraph 196.
57   The Interim Taylor Report, paragraph 250.
58   http://www.guardian.co.uk/media/2004/jul/07/pressandpublishing.football1

Patnick, the only Conservative MP in the area, was not even at the game to witness those events. Nevertheless, his comments were widely used.[59]

Two days after The Sun's story, the Home Secretary inferred in the House of Commons that 19 police officers had been physically assaulted at the ground and that SYP were collating the information to pass on to the inquiry.

However, by May 3rd, following questions from the House, Douglas Hurd was unable to state how those injuries were sustained. No evidence regarding physical assaults on officers was ever passed to the inquiry.[60]

In addition, from the thousands of press pictures taken and the 71 hours of recorded video footage taken from five police cameras, 19 SWFC cameras, as well as BBC footage, there was not one single image or image frame to support the allegation. Taylor completely dismissed this argument saying, *"Not a single witness supported any of those allegations."*[61]

The SYP And SWFC View

While unnamed police officers and SWFC officials continued to infer supporter responsibility to the media, they both conducted their own private investigations into the causes of the Disaster.

SYP argued it was the responsibility of SWFC to monitor the pens and they employed a structural engineer to investigate safety aspects of the terrace, discovering that the numerous breaches to the 'Green Guide' were perhaps even greater than the HSE estimated.[62]

SWFC also produced its own 105-page report. In that report, *"SWFC laid responsibility for monitoring and managing the crowd with the Police and maintained that the sole cause of the Disaster was Duckenfield's blunder in not redirecting fans away from the tunnel after he ordered the gate to be opened. The safety certificate, and all the issues relating to the changes to the pens, barriers and fences, was, the club argued, the City Council's responsibility."*[63]

59   http://www.contrast.org/hillsborough/history/media.shtm
60   http://www.publications.parliament.uk/pa/cm198889/cmhansrd/1989-05-03/Writtens-1.html
61   The Interim Taylor Report, paragraph 257.
62   The Stuart-Smith Scrutiny Report, paragraph 17.
63   David Conn, "The Beautiful Game: Searching the Soul of Football", page 92.

The Supporters' View
LFC supporters have been consistent in their belief that the Disaster was due to a failure of the police's crowd management, coupled with a lack of communication and organisation.[64] In a BBC Radio interview held at the ground, Dr Glynn Phillips spoke of the mayhem outside the ground and said police had *"lost control."*[65]

His view has been echoed by LFC supporters throughout the subsequent years. The supporters' view of police mismanagement is comprehensively supported by the findings of the Taylor Report.

The Taylor Report
On April 17th 1989, Lord Justice Taylor was appointed to conduct a public inquiry. The terms of reference were: *"To inquire into the events at Sheffield Wednesday football ground on April 15th 1989 and to make recommendations about the needs for crowd control and safety at sports events."*

Submitted to the inquiry were 3,776 written statements of evidence and 1,550 letters. Taylor also considered 71 hours of video footage and the oral evidence of 174 witnesses.

On August 4th 1989, the Interim Taylor Report (ITR) was published. In it, Taylor exonerated LFC supporters and *"found the main reason for the Disaster was a failure of police control."*[66]

Taylor found the build-up and crush of fans outside the turnstiles were not the fault of the supporters and the likelihood of problems occurring was highly foreseeable. Once the decision to open Gate C was taken, the appropriate action of closing access to the central pens should have been taken but was not.[67]

64   The Interim Taylor Report, paragraphs 223-225 incl.
65   Rogan Taylor, Andrew Ward, Tim Newburn, "The Day of the Hillsborough Disaster: A Narrative Account", pg 85.
66   The Interim Taylor Report, paragraph 278.
67   The Interim Taylor Report, paragraph 231.

Taylor said that if SYP were not aware of the overcrowding prior to opening the gate then they should have been. Taylor then criticised the slow reaction of police to initiate the Disaster Plan.[68]

Taylor also criticised the FA, Sheffield City Council and SWFC. Regarding SWFC, Taylor said: *"There are a number of respects in which the failure of the club contributed to the disaster."*[69]

Taylor went into great detail specifying all the ways in which the club was at fault. The layout and the confusing signposting ahead of the turnstiles, which contributed to the build-up of supporters, and the poor signposting on the concourse, partially caused the overfilling of the central pens.

The number of ways in which the Leppings Lane terraces breached guidelines was also denounced, with the terrace itself described as *"unsatisfactory"* and *"ill-suited"*[70] to host the number of supporters invited. Taylor said the City Council's failure to revise or amend the safety certificate was a *"serious breach of duty"*,[71] while the FA was criticised for its *"ill-considered choice of venue."*[72]

However, the most damning criticism was reserved for Duckenfield, for *"failing to take effective control"* and SYP's attempts to *"blame supporters for being late and drunk."*[73] Taylor concluded that, although Duckenfield apologised for falsely blaming supporters for causing deaths it was, *"a matter of regret that at the hearing, and in their submissions, the South Yorkshire Police were not prepared to concede that they were in any respect at fault for what had occurred."*[74]

On the day the Taylor Report was released, Duckenfield was suspended from duty, Chief Constable Peter Wright apologised for SYP's role in the Disaster and offered to resign, and his Assistant C.C Ian Daines said: *"Blame has been attributed and some of it, quite rightly, at the feet of South Yorkshire Police and various other organisations."*[75]

---

68   The Interim Taylor Report, paragraph 301.
69   The Interim Taylor Report, paragraph 290.
70   The Interim Taylor Report, paragraph 290.
71   The Interim Taylor Report, paragraph 286.
72   The Interim Taylor Report, paragraph 270.
73 & 74 The Interim Taylor Report, paragraph 285.
75   http://news.bbc.co.uk/2/hi/uk_news/855766.stm

Legal Proceedings

Hillsborough's Cold Case
Between 4:30pm on April 15th and 9:00am on April 16th 1989, two CCTV video tapes were stolen from the SWFC Control Room. It was later concluded that those videos would not have shown anything relevant.[76] However, the important question of why they were stolen in the first place, and by whom, remains unanswered.

The Inquest - Who, Where and When
Just three days after the first anniversary of the Disaster, Dr Popper, the coroner for South Yorkshire, employed by Sheffield City Council, started the statutory process of establishing who each of the deceased was and when and where he or she had died. This was established via a West Midlands police officer reading a summary of undisclosed evidence.

Detailed in each summary were the blood alcohol levels of each victim. These summaries were not subjected to any cross-examinations and were presented as fact.

The Coroner was not meant to deal with the question of how each victim died until the Director of Public Prosecutions (DPP) had decided whether or not prosecutions could be brought against anyone involved.

The DPP
Under the advice of two senior Queens Council officers, the DPP, Allan Green, decided not to bring criminal prosecutions against any individual, group or corporate body for the Disaster. Despite Lord Justice Taylor's findings, the DPP said there was insufficient evidence.

No further explanation for this decision was offered when the announcement was made on August 14th 1990.

The Inquest To Establish 'How?'
The DPP's decision meant that the inquest could now resume establishing how the deceased came to their deaths. The jury had already heard the uncontested view that the victims died quickly, with no pre-death trauma and, as a result, a 3:15pm cut-off point was established. Any evidence or questions over the emergency response then became inadmissible.[77]

---

76   The Stuart-Smith Scrutiny Report, paragraphs 21 & 22.
77   http://www.independent.co.uk/news/uk/home-news/ambulance-ban-cost-lives-at-hillsborough-622239.html

The focus of the inquest was the build-up at the turnstiles and what occurred inside the pens. Witness statements were then read to the court including Superintendent Marshall's 17-page recollection of the day, which contained many unsubstantiated allegations that Taylor dismissed in his own report.

At this point it was demanded that the jury be dismissed and the inquest stopped. Following two days of legal arguments, the Coroner requested that the jury should simply forget those prejudicial comments.

The Coroner then summed up the evidence and gave legal direction to the jury. Jurors were warned they had to be convinced beyond reasonable doubt if they were to return a verdict of unlawful killing and advised that a verdict of accidental death did not equate to 'no blame' and could include a degree of negligence.

The jury went on to return a majority verdict of 9-2 of accidental death.

The Police Complaints Authority
On July 11th 1990, the Police Complaints Authority (PCA) instructed SYP to commence disciplinary proceedings against Duckenfield and Murray.

Murray faced one charge of neglect of duty; Duckenfield faced four charges of neglect of duty and one of discreditable conduct.

In November, Duckenfield resigned from SYP due to ill health. As a direct result, disciplinary action against him could no longer be concluded and SYP decided it was unfair to proceed with action against Murray alone.

The Judicial Review
Bereaved families approached the Attorney General, who has the power to order new inquests, to do just that, as new evidence had come to light. The Attorney General refused. Six families were granted a judicial review at the divisional court to quash the original inquest verdict, based on the irregular way evidence was presented and the emergence of new evidence.

The divisional court dismissed their application.

In its final judgment, the High Court even refers to the UK's biggest sporting disaster as having occurred at *"an FA Cup semi-final match between Liverpool Football Club and Sheffield Wednesday Football Club."*[78]

---

78   http://www.liverpoolfc.tv/club/docs/chronology.doc

Civil Cases

Civil cases have been brought throughout the period since the Disaster. The Chief Constable of SYP has not contested liability for these claims. In a House of Lords judgment, Lord Keith concluded that the Chief Constable *"has admitted liability in negligence in respect of the deaths and physical injuries."*[79] Subsequent civil compensation payments to the bereaved and injured were issued jointly by SYP, SWFC and Sheffield City Council.

The Scrutiny

In December 1996, the TV documentary, 'Hillsborough', claimed new evidence had come to light. Newspapers carried the story and public interest in the Disaster was once again stirred; a demand for a new inquiry followed.

Instead, a 'scrutiny of evidence' was ordered by Home Secretary Jack Straw and on June 30th 1997, Lord Justice Stuart-Smith was appointed to oversee proceedings. A scrutiny has no basis in law and, unlike an inquiry, is not a public hearing. No cross examination of contentious evidence occurs. Stuart-Smith would objectively assess all evidence presented to him, unchallenged and in private.

When the scrutiny began it appeared that Lord Justice Stuart-Smith had pre-conceived ideas about the Disaster. When arriving at Liverpool's Maritime Museum on October 6th 1997 to visit some of the families, he asked one bereaved father: *"Have you got a few of your people or are they like the Liverpool fans, turn up at the last minute?"*[80]

Stuart-Smith went on to assess new evidence that was not forwarded to the inquiry or the inquests. Stuart-Smith also considered the contentious 3:15pm cut-off point, potential interference with witnesses, and edited witness statements for his report. He upheld Taylor's findings but he did not believe the new evidence warranted a new inquest.

He concluded: *"None of the evidence I was asked to consider added anything significant to the evidence which was available to Lord Taylor's inquiry or to the inquests."*[81]

Jack Straw accepted the findings, stating there were no grounds to order either a new inquiry or inquest.

79   The Stuart-Smith Scrutiny Report, chapter 1, paragraph 10 & 64, plus Divisional Court transcript page 40, Lord Keith of Kinkel in "Alcock v Chief Constable, 1992 ac 310, 392."
80   http://www.liverpoolfc.tv/club/docs/chronology.doc
81   The Stuart-Smith Scrutiny Report, Chapter 7, paragraph 6.

In November 1998, Professor Phil Scraton was granted access to the House of Lords Reading Room. There he examined numerous transcripts of the meetings between Stuart-Smith and the relevant parties. From this examination it seems that a draft of the report was circulated in advance to people who were likely to be criticised. It appeared that they were allowed to comment on the draft before it went to print.

In the draft report, Stuart-Smith had expressed concern that several witness statements had been altered to edit out any comments that were adverse to SYP, but comments detrimental to the supporters had been left in. There was, however, little mention of this concern in Stuart-Smith's final report. He simply says it *"would have been better"*[82] had some of the deletions not been made and it was at worse an *"error of judgement."*[83]

The Police Statements
In 1998 the Home Office made available the statements taken by police officers on the day of the Disaster. These statements show the extent to which they were edited.

Critical comments from on-duty PCs, relating to a lack of leadership by senior officers, poor communication or comments on how crowd control tactics differed from previous years, were altered or edited out entirely.

Family lawyers estimate that 183 PC statements were subject to such editing. Many PCs refused to sign the altered statements put to them.[84 & 85]

The Private Prosecution
In August 1998 the Hillsborough Family Support Group commenced private prosecutions against Duckenfield and Murray. They were charged with two offences: manslaughter and wilful malfeasance in public office.

A further charge of perverting the course of justice was filed in direct relation to Duckenfield's lie about Liverpool supporters allegedly forcing open Gate C.

After two years of legal wrangling, a case was finally put to a jury in Leeds, West Yorkshire, and lasted for six weeks. On July 21st 2000, after four days of deliberation, the jury found Murray not guilty of manslaughter. Four days later the jury announced it could not reach a verdict on Duckenfield.

82 & 83   The Stuart-Smith Scrutiny Report, Chapter 4, paragraph 89.
84   http://news.bbc.co.uk/1/hi/uk/839047.stm
85   http://www.telegraph.co.uk/htmlContent.jhtml?html=/archive/1999/02/28/nhil28.html

•

The jury, when asked, indicated that, with a little more time, they may reach a majority verdict. Mr Justice Hooper decided against this and also refused a retrial.

He told the court that forcing Mr Duckenfield to undergo another trial would constitute clear oppression and the trial had already been very public and the defendants had faced public humiliation.

He also added, *"I have an overriding duty to ensure a fair trial for the defendant. That, I am firmly convinced, is no longer possible."*[86]

For his own part, Murray admitted in court that he was haunted by the memory of Hillsborough and wished that, at the time, it had occurred to him to close access to the tunnel.

---

86   http://news.bbc.co.uk/2/hi/uk_news/855766.stm

Hope For Hillsborough

Bereaved parent Anne Williams is actively pursuing a case in the European Court of Human Rights, challenging the official version of the circumstances under which her 15-year-old son, Kevin Daniel Williams, died.

Anne believes that the original Inquest was unsatisfactory in establishing the true cause of her son's death and that, subsequently, the information on his death certificate is incorrect.

Anne argues that any cut-off point violates the right to investigate fully all the circumstances surrounding her son's death, under Section 2 of the Human Rights Act.

She also argues that if a jury is not presented with all available facts then Section 6, The Right to a Fair Trial, is also violated.

There is eyewitness evidence from medically-qualified personnel to demonstrate that Kevin was alive after the official 3:15pm cut-off time. With simple medical attention, it is believed his life could have been saved.

Evidence has also been submitted which details how the bereaved families' right to a fair trial at the original inquest was also impeded.

However, a favourable verdict for Anne Williams will not automatically precipitate a new inquest. The European Court of Human Rights has no judicial power over the British Government and it would be up to the incumbent Home Secretary to authorise a new inquest.

That said, if the European Courts do decide that there is a case to be heard, it would be official confirmation that the original inquest was unsatisfactory.

This recognition would place pressure on the Home Secretary to open a new inquest, so that all the circumstances surrounding the Disaster could finally be established beyond question.

At the time of writing, a decision from the European Courts was imminent.

Timeline For April 15th 1989

12:00 noon Supporters start to arrive at Leppings Lane/outside the ground.

2:00pm Duckenfield and Murray go to Police Control Room.

2:30 to 2:40pm Large concentration of supporters bottlenecked outside the turnstile area.

2:38pm Strong surge along dividing fence enclosing pens 3 & 4.

2:39pm Boy carried out through Gate C.

2:40pm Request sent to Police Control to send spare mounted officers to Leppings Lane End. Announcement on tannoy system asks people to move forward. Further surge in pens 3 & 4.

2:42pm Radio system develops fault for several minutes.

2:47pm Request from Marshall to open gates at Leppings Lane End.

2:48pm Gate C opened to eject supporter. Others enter before gate C closed again.

2:50pm Pens 3 & 4 are full. Inspector Sewell deploys 60 officers to the track, the West Stand and Gate A.

2:51pm Football teams announced over the tannoy.

2:52pm Message from Marshall that people outside might be killed if gates are not opened. Gate C opened on Duckenfield's orders, allowing 2,000 supporters to enter.

2:54pm Teams come on to the pitch.

2:57pm Gate C closed again.

2:59pm People in the pens start climbing over the perimeter fence to escape the crush.

3:00pm The match kicks off. Call from Constable Waugh at SYP HQ asking if ambulances required. Answer no. Gate 1 opened to allow supporters into enclosure. Jackson sees supporters on pitch and goes up to the Police Control Room to report.

3:04pm Beardsley strikes the crossbar at the Kop end. Inevitable surge in the pens.

3:05pm Crush barrier towards the front of pen 3 gives way, causing supporters to fall over.

3:06pm Match stopped by referee when Greenwood approaches him on the pitch. Murray radios for a fleet of ambulances.

3:10pm Jackson asked to confirm Operation Support by Force Incident Room. Request to Control from perimeter fence for bolt cutters.

3:13pm First ambulance (from St. John's) comes on to the pitch at the North East corner and drives to the perimeter fence close to gate 3. Requests for cutting gear and for the fire brigade made by Bichard, who is then informed that supporters had forced Gate C.

3:17pm Kelly, Kirton and Mackrell go to the Control Room for information. Duckenfield says he thinks there are fatalities and the game is likely to be abandoned. He also says there has been an inrush of supporters and that Gate C had been forced open.

3:17pm Ambulances begin to arrive at the Penistone Rd entrance.

3:20pm Second ambulance enters the ground.

3:22pm Fire Brigade turns up at both Leppings Lane & Penistone Rd and is told by a police inspector, *"I don't think we really need you."*

3:29pm Requests made for doctors and nurses at the ground.

3:30pm Meeting in the club boardroom with Duckenfield, Jackson, Kelly, the match referee and representatives of the three clubs. Duckenfield indicates that the match is likely to be abandoned.

3:35pm Detective Chief Superintendent Addis makes contact via telephone with Control.

3:35-3:36pm Edwards' ambulance enters the ground.

3:40pm BBC Radio Two: *"Unconfirmed reports are that a door was broken at the end that was holding LFC supporters."*

4:30pm Last casualties leave the ground.

5:15pm Duckenfield and Jackson travel to SYP HQ.

5:45pm Chief Constable Peter Wright and his deputy meet Duckenfield and Jackson.

Between 4:30pm on April 15th and 9:00am on April 16th Two CCTV tapes are stolen from ground's Police Control Room. The crime and motive remain unsolved.

Glossary

Further information on The Hillsborough Disaster can be obtained from the following sources, which you are encouraged to read:

Books & Articles
No Last Rights: The Denial of Justice and the Promotion of Myth in the Aftermath of the Hillsborough Disaster
Phil Scraton, Ann Jemphrey & Sheila Coleman, ISBN 0-904517-30-6

Hillsborough: The Truth
Phil Scraton; ISBN 1-84018-156-7

Death on the Terraces: The Contexts and Injustices of the 1989 Hillsborough Disaster
Phil Scraton in P. Darby et al (eds) Soccer and Disaster: International Perspectives ISBN 0-7146-8289-6

Policing with Contempt: The Degrading of Truth and Denial of Justice in the Aftermath of the Hillsborough Disaster'
Phil Scraton, Journal of Law and Society, 1999 vol 26, no 3, pp273-297

Power, Conflict and Criminalisation
Phil Scraton, London: Routledge (Ch 4 'Negligence without liability': the scale of injustice after Hillsborough), 2007

The Day of the Hillsborough Disaster
Rogan Taylor, Andrew Ward, Tim Newburn (Eds.), ISBN 0-85323-199-0

When You Walk Through the Storm
Sean Smith & Anne Williams, ISBN 9781840180671

The Lost Afternoon
The Guardian, April 11th 1999,
http://www.guardian.co.uk/theobserver/1999/apr/11/featuresreview.review6

Reports
The Hillsborough Stadium Disaster, 15 April 1989: Inquiry by Lord Justice Taylor
(Cm.: 765) Peter Taylor ISBN 0-10-107652-5

The Hillsborough Stadium Disaster: Inquiry Final Report (Command Paper)
Home Office; ISBN 0-10-109622-4
(Both reports can be downloaded from the following website http://en.wikipedia.org/wiki/ Taylor_Report)

Scrutiny of Evidence Relating to the Hillsborough Football Stadium Disaster (Command Paper)
Home Office; ISBN 0-10-138782-2

The Taylor Inquiry and Stuart-Smith Scrutiny of Evidence can be read here
www.southyorks.police.uk/foi/information_classes/categories/

Sports Stadia After Hillsborough: Seminar Papers
RIBA, Sports Council, Owen Luder (Ed.) ISBN 0-947877-72-X

Ground safety and public order: Hillsborough Stadium Disaster, report of Joint Working Party on Ground Safety and Public Order (Report/Joint Executive on Football Safety)
Joint Working Party on Ground Safety and Public Order; ISBN 0-901783-73-0

Health & Safety Executive reports into the Hillsborough Disaster
www.hse.gov.uk/foi/releases/hillsborough.htm

Hillsborough Attitudes Survey Report
www.liv.ac.uk/footballindustry/attitude.html

Websites

Official website of the Hillsborough Family Support Group (HFSG)
www.hfsg.co.uk

Official website of the Hillsborough Justice Campaign (HJC)
www.contrast.org/hillsborough/

Anne Williams' personal campaign website;
www.hopeforhillsborough.piczo.com/?cr=6

BBC News On this Day
http://news.bbc.co.uk/onthisday/hi/dates/stories/april/15/newsid_2491000/2491195.stm

Wikipedia
http://en.wikipedia.org/wiki/Hillsborough_disaster

Google
www.google.co.uk/search?sourceid=navclient&ie=UTF-8&rlz=1T4GFRD_en___GB253&q=the+hillsborough+disaster

Media

'Hillsborough', a Granada Television drama from 1996 (Jimmy McGovern)
http://www.imdb.com/title/tt0116533/

How the disaster was reported
www.fanatical.hu/hillsborough-disaster-tragedy-1989-liverpool-video/

Report on how SYP statements were altered
www.wsws.org/articles/1999/mar1999/foot-m10.shtml

External Links

'Stand Up Sit Down' (SUSD) (The organisation to introduce safe standing areas in top-flight English football)
www.standupsitdown.co.uk

The Football Licensing Authority
www.flaweb.org.uk/search/flasearch.php?zoom_query=HILLSBOROUGH&zoom_and=0

Crowd Dynamics
www.crowddynamics.com

John Alfred Anderson (62)
Colin Mark Ashcroft (19)
James Gary Aspinall (18)
Kester Roger Marcus Ball (16)
Gerard Bernard Patrick Baron (67)
Simon Bell (17)
Barry Sidney Bennett (26)
David John Benson (22)
David William Birtle (22)
Tony Bland (22)
Paul David Brady (21)
Andrew Mark Brookes (26)
Carl Brown (18)
David Steven Brown (25)
Henry Thomas Burke (47)
Peter Andrew Burkett (24)
Paul William Carlile (19)
Raymond Thomas Chapman (50)
Gary Christopher Church (19)
Joseph Clark (29)
Paul Clark (18)
Gary Collins (22)
Stephen Paul Copoc (20)
Tracey Elizabeth Cox (23)
James Philip Delaney (19)
Christopher Barry Devonside (18)
Christopher Edwards (29)
Vincent Michael Fitzsimmons (34)
Thomas Steven Fox (21)
Jon-Paul Gilhooley (10)
Barry Glover (27)
Ian Thomas Glover (20)
Derrick George Godwin (24)
Roy Harry Hamilton (34)
Philip Hammond (14)
Eric Hankin (33)
Gary Harrison (27)
Stephen Francis Harrison (31)
Peter Andrew Harrison (15)
David Hawley (39)
James Robert Hennessy (29)
Paul Anthony Hewitson (26)
Carl Darren Hewitt (17)
Nicholas Michael Hewitt (16)
Sarah Louise Hicks (19)
Victoria Jane Hicks (15)
Gordon Rodney Horn (20)
Arthur Horrocks (41)

Thomas Howard (39)
Thomas Anthony Howard (14)
Eric George Hughes (42)
Alan Johnston (29)
Christine Anne Jones (27)
Gary Philip Jones (18)
Richard Jones (25)
Nicholas Peter Joynes (27)
Anthony Peter Kelly (29)
Michael David Kelly (38)
Carl David Lewis (18)
David William Mather (19)
Brian Christopher Mathews (38)
Francis Joseph McAllister (27)
John McBrien (18)
Marion Hazel McCabe (21)
Joseph Daniel McCarthy (21)
Peter McDonnell (21)
Alan McGlone (28)
Keith McGrath (17)
Paul Brian Murray (14)
Lee Nicol (14)
Stephen Francis O'Neill (17)
Jonathon Owens (18)
William Roy Pemberton (23)
Carl William Rimmer (21)
David George Rimmer (38)
Graham John Roberts (24)
Steven Joseph Robinson (17)
Henry Charles Rogers (17)
Colin Andrew Hugh William Sefton (23)
Inger Shah (38)
Paula Ann Smith (26)
Adam Edward Spearritt (14)
Philip John Steele (15)
David Leonard Thomas (23)
Patrik John Thompson (35)
Peter Reuben Thompson (30)
Stuart Paul William Thompson (17)
Peter Francis Tootle (21)
Christopher James Traynor (26)
Martin Kevin Traynor (16)
Kevin Tyrrell (15)
Colin Wafer (19)
Ian David Whelan (19)
Martin Kenneth Wild (29)
Kevin Daniel Williams (15)
Graham John Wright (17)